The A
College Admissions
Almanac

How to Get into a Top 20 University While Still Having a Life

Written by Nathan Halberstadt, author of *New SAT Strategies for a 1600*

Edited by Varun Tekur

Thanks to contributors Eric Tarlin, Jordan Cline, and William Cuozzo

The Authentic College Admissions Almanac: How to Get into a Top 20 University While Still Having a Life

Author: Nathan Halberstadt
Editor: Varun Tekur
Contributor: William Cuozzo
Contributor: Eric Tarlin
Contributor: Jordan Cline
Cover Designer: Nathan Halberstadt

Printed in the United States of America
First Printing, 2018
ISBN: 9781717935311

amazon.com/author/nathanhalberstadt

CONTENTS

Section IV: Enjoying Your High School Years

Chapter 13: Cashing in on Summer

Chapter 14: Sleep in High School

Chapter 15: Having a Life

Chapter 16: Final Timeline

Introduction

Why Should I Read This Book?

Overture

This book will teach you how to navigate the college admissions process without letting it dictate your life. The process exists to serve you, not you to serve the process. The meaning of your life is not determined by this process. It's not about sucking the soul out of your teen years. It's not a monster. The mechanism of matching students with colleges is beneficial for you and for society as a whole; you just have to look at it with the right perspective. This book will encourage you to live your life to the fullest while at the same time showing you what you can and should do to connect your current life to the next major stage in your life: college.

Why Listen to This Advice?

I wasn't an A+ student. In fact, I cruised through high school with quite a few B grades. I'm no star athlete or extraordinary individual, yet I managed to get accepted into a number of top universities including Vanderbilt University, where I will be attending this fall. My good friends who I collaborated with while writing this book are current students at Harvard, MIT, Harvard (again), and Columbia. My older brother studied engineering at Stanford University, and the editor of this book is himself a Harvard man. The contributor from Columbia also works for Columbia University Admissions, so he is definitely an authority on this subject. We've all done quite well in the college admissions process by following a certain set of guidelines (one could even call them "rules for life") that I will outline in this book.

Now that we've gotten that not-so-humble-brag out of the way, let me be clear: this book is not going to tell you to become someone with no life who does nothing but sit in their room and study. Those kids will never get into a top college. Instead, this book will teach you the steps you need to take in order to get into a top 20 university while having a fun time along the way.

Why Aim for the Top 20?

Some people probably aren't overly worried about the caliber of school that they attend, and that's ok. There's nothing wrong with not attending a top 20 university. But if you do go to a top school, you will be guaranteed access to amazing teachers, classmates, facilities, financial aid, internships, research opportunities, organizations, and jobs. This isn't to say that you can't do well at a school that isn't highly ranked. On the contrary, there are amazing teachers at most universities, and if you work hard, you can be a star at any college and do incredibly well in life. However, if you go to a top university, more opportunities will be available to you, which in itself should be great a reason to do your best and attempt to get into the best college possible.

Who This Book Is For?

I'm going to walk you through each of the different aspects of high school academic and extracurricular life and explain the must-dos and must-don'ts of high school. If you're just starting high school, you will find this book helpful as a roadmap for the years ahead. And if you're already in the college admissions process, this book is also perfect for you because you are in the midst of making many of the decisions I'll be talking about.

The Goal

My hope for you is that you strive to do your absolute best and that you get into your dream school. Although it may be harder to get into a top 20 school if you haven't lived up to your potential in the past, don't worry! Nobody is perfect! This book will help you do the best you can even with a bit of a shaky track record. It's definitely not too late to get accepted into great colleges and to get great scholarships. So, don't count yourself out! And for those of you who are driven, high-performing students, schools like Harvard and MIT are well within reach if you persevere and follow the trajectory of excellence laid out in this book.

Section I: Inside the Classroom

Chapter 1

Choosing the Right Classes

Although two different applicants may both have straight-A grades, the strength of each of their applications is determined by a factor that goes beyond the individual letter grades on their transcript—the types of classes that they take. People may tell you that "An A is an A, and a B is a B". But in reality, the people who read your college applications will view your grades differently based on the specific classes that you have taken.

What Class Difficulty Level to Take

Most schools tend to have a ranking of classes in each subject categorized by level of difficulty, usually something along the lines of College Prep, Honors, and AP from easiest to hardest. Schools obviously have different names for these levels of difficulty, but the idea is similar across the board. You may wonder what level you should take. Should you take the less challenging College Prep classes and get the easy A? Or should you take the honors and AP classes even if there is a chance of getting a B? The answer depends on your goals and your personality.

If your goal is to get into your local state school and to just get by academically without too much sweat or stress (no shame in that, everybody is different), then take the College Prep level classes and get perfect grades (i.e. making the NBA All-Star team by racking up empty stats like Carmelo Anthony on the Knicks). Getting straight-A grades in easy classes is a sure way to get into your state school with flying colors. Better yet, you will definitely be able to have a life. Imagine going home after school and not having to stress about difficult tests and homework problems. Sounds like the life, right? And for some people, this legitimately is the right choice.

But for the more driven, high-performing students, I would 100% recommend that you always choose the highest level classes even if it means struggling to get the A grade. It's going to be difficult, but these classes will force you to grow and to stretch your academic boundaries. Taking the most challenging classes—and taking lots of them—forces you to get better at managing your time and learning new material. It's like practicing in a sport against someone who is more talented than you (like a rookie Jayson Tatum stepping up to face Lebron James in the playoffs)—it makes you better. Let's make a little analogy here. I'm a tennis player. It's common knowledge in tennis that if you always play against people worse than you, you won't get any better, and you might even get worse at tennis. But if you play against people better than you, you will grow to become as good as they are. Same with school. If you take the hardest classes with the smartest students, you will learn to handle challenging tasks and become smarter. You will learn how to study (enabling you to be a lifelong learner), how to learn from your mistakes (allowing you to develop your emotional intelligence), and how to be more ready to face challenges and opportunities in the future. And after all, isn't that what school is about?

Obviously, there is a point at which you are just overwhelming yourself; if you are going to get a C or lower in a difficult class, it's not worth taking. But I would encourage you to push yourself each year in high school. Most schools allow students to switch down to a lower-level class in the first few weeks of school. Take advantage of the challenge of higher-level classes while knowing that you can always drop to a lower-level if needed. Don't limit yourself by not signing up to take any difficult classes.

The Benefits of Tough Classes

During my senior year, I ended up taking five AP classes. Was it tough? Of course! But it forced me to become a more knowledgeable and inquisitive student. An important thing to remember is that pushing yourself by taking difficult courses will pay off tremendously in the long run. For example, if I had taken easy classes in high school, I don't think that I would have developed the necessary skills to get a high-quality SAT score. Further, my SAT Subject Test scores would have been lower because I would not have learned the necessary material to ace them. And I wouldn't have had any AP scores to send to colleges because I would have only taken College Prep and Honors classes. So if you're aiming for a top college, taking the hardest courses possible is a no-brainer.

Selecting Specific Subjects

As far as which subjects to enroll in during high school, you must absolutely take a legitimate course in math, science, and English every year. That means taking math courses like algebra 2, geometry, statistics, and calculus; The same goes for science. You must take biology, chemistry, and physics. Classes like oceanography (fish class), zoology, and anatomy may be fun, but colleges will not consider those courses replacements for the core sciences. You need to take an English class every year to continue to develop your reading and writing ability no matter how much you hate it. Also, keep in mind that your English teachers will be happy to help you with your college essays, so stay on friendly terms with them. I would recommend taking a foreign language all four years, but it's not the biggest deal if you drop your foreign language for your senior year to take something more interesting. The same goes for history. Take core history classes for at least your first three years of high school and then maybe take something you're more interested in during your senior year.

As far as elective courses, feel free to take courses in subject areas that you are interested in such as photography, band, computer science, orchestra, economics, clothing, foods, choir, law, drama, TV, or whatever! But you should probably limit those interests to one class, and definitely not more than two, a year. I took band and my editor took computer science throughout high school. Besides the fact that we really enjoyed these subjects, our electives showed colleges there was something other than just traditional academic subjects that we were passionate about. Also, our electives and extracurriculars (musical activities and robotics, respectively) created a cohesive area of interest. You should consider doing the same in some elective area.

Chapter 2

Nailing the Transcript

Chasing Perfection

What you've heard is true: you need pretty much straight-A grades in order to get into Ivy League caliber schools. Of course, there are exceptions, and many other variables come into play besides grades, but you must do everything in your power to keep your grades as high as possible. If you are aiming for the top 20 schools in the nation, almost all of your legitimate competitors will have straight-A grades.

If in the process of challenging yourself academically, you get a sprinkling of B grades, it's not the end of the world, but you might have to aim a little lower than Harvard. Can I let you in on a little secret? I was accepted into Vanderbilt University even though I received 7 B grades throughout high school (3 of which were B minuses). Not exactly perfection. If those B grades had been A grades, I definitely could have been Harvard or Stanford material. Friends of mine who are going to Ivy League schools submitted applications on the whole similar to mine—only they had perfect transcripts. Therefore, grades really do matter. Again, the only major difference between them and me was that they had straight-A grades, and I didn't. That's probably one reason why they went to the Ivy League, and I didn't. Now, I do absolutely love the school that I am going to (Anchor Down!!!), and I honestly couldn't be happier, but it's important to realize that your grades do have consequences.

Grades in Perspective

So here's what you need to focus on: shoot for straight-A grades. But if it doesn't happen, don't beat yourself up too much. You might not be able to get into Harvard or Stanford, but you could still have a great shot at getting into other top 20 universities like Duke, Vanderbilt, or Northwestern. Just make sure you never get C grades or anything lower. When top colleges see that, they will immediately think you are either unintelligent or slacking, both of which are not ideal conclusions. However, if a university's admissions committee sees A grades with a sprinkling of B grades in tough classes, they will assume that you work hard and are willing to challenge yourself even if you aren't perfect. And if you have a stray low grade here or there throughout high school, keep in mind the big picture. It's not the worst thing that could happen to you, but do better next time.

Grades Aren't the Only Component of Your Application

Some students believe that grades are the only part of the application that matters, and that's just not true. There are many straight-A students, even ones that I have known in the communities around me, who earned straight-A grades but got rejected from almost every school they applied to except for their safety schools. Now, that's not to say that these students won't succeed, but my point here is that there is clearly a lot more to the admissions process than your grades. If you have the grades, but you are missing certain other key elements that I will go over later on in this book, you will get rejected. We all know lots of really smart students with perfect transcripts who got rejected from top colleges. Don't be one of those kids.

Keep in mind that colleges do tend to read your transcript with a grain of salt. Simply put, the amount of effort and ability required to get an A in one school might barely get you a C in a different school. Different schools have different levels of difficulty. Further, different classes and teachers within the same school require different levels of effort. So colleges have to use some other method, such as standardized test scores, to put the grades in perspective. For example, if a student has straight-A grades and an SAT score of only 1200, the college admissions committee will immediately conclude that you went to an easy school, took easy classes, chose easy teachers, and got easy A grades. The admissions committee will decide that you don't make the cut because your poor SAT score partially nullifies your high GPA. On the other hand, if you have B grades but a near perfect SAT score, colleges will assume that you challenged yourself in school and took the hardest classes to push yourself. In that case, they will at least consider you.

Colleges want students who are accomplished and have done big things, not just people with pristine grades. Even if you have a 4.0 GPA and a perfect A+ transcript, you still need to do something outside of the classroom that is impressive. In the chapters that follow, we will go through these different ways to stand out from the pack.

Chapter 3

Acing Your Standardized Tests

Importance

Test scores are *incredibly* important. Just like your grades, they are one of the quantitative litmus tests of your application. Because these tests are nationally standardized, they give colleges the opportunity to do something that they would never be able to do with just your grades—compare all applicants on the same scale. If you score in the 99th percentile on a big exam like the SAT or ACT, it tells universities that you have outperformed ninety-nine out of every one-hundred people taking the test. Game over. End of story. There's no negotiation here like there is with grades. You have to do well on your standardized tests.

As I stated earlier, if you have high grades but really low test scores, colleges assume your high school curriculum was too easy, so they will not accept you. On the flip side, if you have high test scores but less than perfect grades, they will assume you are challenging yourself academically and might consider you for a spot in spite of your grades. Yet, naive students regularly pull all-nighters for an extra point or two in a class while stupidly not preparing for tests like the SAT or ACT. Don't treat the SAT or ACT like a half court shot you just have to hope will go in; you should be more intentional than that. Set yourself up for a slam-dunk on these standardized tests.

Colleges will never tell you this, but your SAT or ACT score (depending on which one you take) is almost as important as your entire high school transcript. They can't tell you this because then students would stop trying in school, but colleges really can't tell the whole story from just the grades on your transcript. As long as your grades are solid, they will look at a number of different elements of your application, including your SAT or ACT score, in order to really decide if you are smart enough to make the cut.

PSAT/NMSQT

Before we get into a discussion about mastering the SAT, we should talk about an often-overlooked test that can boost your application if you do well on it: the PSAT/NMSQT. The PSAT/NMSQT is one of the least talked about exams, but it's incredibly important if you are a high-performing student because it serves as a qualification exam for the National Merit Scholarship.

Many students take the exam at the beginning of sophomore year and/or junior year. If you are a top-notch student and think you're within striking distance of getting a National Merit Scholarship, it is definitely worth preparing for the exam. The PSAT/NMSQT is essentially the SAT with an easier pool of questions. By preparing for the PSAT/NMSQT, you are taking out two birds with one stone. I would honestly recommend getting ready for the PSAT/NMSQT using SAT questions because this will force you to work with a harder set of questions, which will prepare you more than adequately for the exam. Take some practice SAT and PSAT/NMSQT exams, go over your mistakes, analyze your weaknesses, and then address those weaknesses in order to improve.

Now, let's address the benefits of doing well on this test. If you score well enough (the standard varies by state and year), you can either be named a National Merit Semifinalist or a Commended Scholar. Being named a Commended Scholar is an honor that you definitely would want to put on your application, but being named a Semifinalist is when you begin to have a shot at the real benefits of doing well on the test. Semifinalists can send an application and their SAT scores to the Scholarship Program. The group of Semifinalists is then narrowed down to a group of Finalists, and eventually to the scholarship winners.

National Merit Scholars can access corporate scholarships as well as the $2,500 National Merit Scholarship. Some schools will even offer full-rides to students who are National Merit Scholars. Additionally, winning any of these scholarships is an accomplishment that will identify you as one of the most elite students in the nation.

Simply having a high enough PSAT/NMSQT score to enter the competition can allow you to get thousands of dollars of scholarship money and can add an additional improvement to your application, so there is no reason to slack-off and miss this opportunity by not preparing.

SAT

If you prepared well for the PSAT/NMSQT, the SAT shouldn't be too much of a challenge. Don't listen to anybody who tells you that the SAT is like an IQ test and that you can't master the exam. That's false. That's literally more false than saying that the earth is flat (hate to break it to any of you fledgling flat earth society members).

I improved my SAT score by 240 points, and I've helped several of my friends do the same. For the SAT, just like anything else in life, practice is key. You should take at least 12 full practice tests before you go take the real SAT. You might think, "that's overkill. Nobody has time for that." But remember, the SAT is extremely valuable—just like your transcript. And it's only one test, whereas your transcript is composed of many classes, tests, and assignments over the course of four years. Thus, the SAT—this one test—is about 100x more important than any individual test you've taken in high school. Think about how many hours you put into making sure your grades are good. Kids stress about one test in one class on their transcript, but then they don't seem to care to prepare for the SAT at all. Don't be like them! Work hard to make your SAT score the best it can possibly be. It won't kill you to put a few hundred hours into practicing for a test that will help secure opportunities for your future. It's the principle of delayed gratification: labor now so that you can reap the rewards ten-fold down the road.

As far as tips and tricks for the SAT, I have a large number of specific strategies that I discovered while I was preparing to take the exam and that others have found incredibly useful. However, I'm not going to give away my secret sauce here because that isn't the focus of this book. If you would like further help on how to master the SAT, I published a book called *New SAT Strategies for a 1600* that details my advice for maximizing your score. The book has received numerous positive reviews, and I have received email feedback from many readers who have told me that my method has improved their score tremendously. So go check it out!

ACT

I never took the ACT, but this test can be a great option for some students to take instead of, or in addition to, the SAT. I reached out to a good friend of mine, William Cuozzo, who is an absolute genius going to MIT and a perfect scorer on the ACT. He has contributed some amazing advice below for any of you considering taking the ACT:

For people struggling to score well on the ACT, it's worth the time to actually learn the skills the test is trying to assess. For example, if you don't understand geometry, you're going to have to learn geometry concepts before you will start scoring well. However, for those of you who are already doing well on practice tests, just continue to practice very specifically for the test. Any moment you have enough time to do a practice section in the months before the test, take it, and then really ramp it up the week or two before. I did five practice tests the week before the ACT because I got this competitive surge of motivation as the test approached. When you do as many practice tests as I did, you build the necessary mental endurance to not make dumb mistakes, you get your pacing down (the ACT is generally a little faster than SAT but with easier questions), and you notice any last weaknesses to fix before exam day.

Another tip: taking the test at your school or at another building you are comfortable in can help your score. Finally, my general advice on standardized testing is to take the ACT and SAT each once, and then take the one you did better on (or think you can do a lot better on) again.

As far as the format of the ACT, there are 5 sections, each with subsections:

- English: 45 minutes, 75 questions
- Math: 60 minutes, 60 questions
- Reading: 35 minutes, 40 questions

- Science: 35 minutes, 40 questions

- Essay (optional): 40 minutes, 1 question

Let me give you some specific tips for each section, starting with the English section in which you read through passages and correct mistakes. This section is definitely the hardest to finish because there are so many questions in such a short amount of time, so you do have to move very quickly. Don't spend too much time on questions that confuse you. Keep moving! Fortunately, the English section focuses on a lot of common sense grammar usage material, and most questions won't seem too hard. One more useful tip on this section is that sometimes all the answer choices make grammatical sense, but one is just more concise. Unless there is a clear reason not to, always pick the shortest answer choice in these cases. Here are some things you must know in order to succeed on this section:

- Punctuation (commas, apostrophes, colons, semicolons, dashes, periods, question marks, and exclamation points)

- Grammar and Usage (subject-verb agreement, pronoun agreement, pronoun forms and cases, adjectives, adverbs, verb forms, comparative and superlative modifiers, and idioms)

- Sentence Structure (independent vs dependent clauses, run-on or fused sentences, comma splices, sentence fragments, misplaced modifiers, shifts in verb tense or voice, and shifts in pronoun person or number)

- Strategy (adding, revising, or deleting sentences; how a sentence fits with the purpose, audience, and focus of a paragraph or the essay as a whole)

- Organization (opening, transitional, and closing phrases or statements; order and focus of sentences or paragraphs)

- Style (tone, clarity, and effectiveness; eliminating ambiguity, wordiness, and redundant material; clarifying vague or awkward material)

Now, let's talk about the math section. This section can be a real time-crunch especially if you are pacing yourself 1 minute per question. However, this is not a good idea because there are more difficult problems at the end that you might need to bank some time for. There is certainly nothing in this section past pre-calculus difficulty. You'll focus mostly on pre-algebra, elementary algebra, intermediate algebra, coordinate geometry, plane geometry, and trigonometry, but there are going to be questions asked in ways you haven't seen before, and you might be tempted to spend too much time on any one such question. As with all tests, keep moving and come back if there's time at the end.

The reading section is the hardest section for most people. You're going to read passages and answer questions about the passages. I advise that you find direct evidence in the passages to answer your questions. Don't guess based on your feelings in the moment. However, for the questions where you have to discern an implication, you just have to use your best intuition from the practice you've done. That's why you need to practice. Also, try to move faster on these in order to save time for the paired-passages. On the paired-passage section, my best tip is to do the questions just relating to passage 1 first after you read it, then the questions just relating to passage 2 after you've just read that, and only then moving on to the questions comparing the two.

The science section requires very little background knowledge. The answers are almost always found in the explanation of the experiment/scenario or in the graphical interpretation of the results. The trouble with this is that, depending on how fast you can read, it can be tough to read everything and still have time to answer the questions. For this section, it is sometimes worth reading the questions first and then quickly looking for the answers in the explanation.

Now let's talk about the ACT essay. The essay is optional, but you should 100% do it. There is no reason not to. You are already there in the building and most colleges want to see an essay score even though they probably won't care too much about what the score is (as long as it is good). I won't go into detail here about how to write an ACT essay, but basically just write a quality essay. Unlike most other essays, your intro/thesis and conclusion matter a little more than the body paragraphs because the intro and conclusion are what scorers see first and last when they have to grade an endless pile of essays. So make a great first and last impression.

SAT Subject Tests

Besides the big college admissions exams like the SAT and ACT, there are also SAT Subject Tests that score your ability in specific academic fields. I recommend that you submit at least 2 subject tests to colleges. This means that throughout high school, if there is a class that you excel in, take the subject test at the end of the year. Take one to two subject tests per year. If you don't get a great score, no worries, you'll have chances to do better the next year. Submit your highest scores only.

Taking an SAT subject test in a subject area right after an AP class that you did well in is a great idea. You will do a majority of the preparation for the AP exam in May, and then you can take a month to brush up and practice specifically for the SAT Subject Test in June.

You will probably want to submit subject test scores in differing areas. For example, submit the Math 2 subject test and the US History subject test. Or maybe submit the Biology test, Spanish test, and the Literature test. Science, Technology, Engineering, and Math (STEM) majors are generally required to submit 1 math and 1 science subject test, so you should absolutely take at least one science SAT Subject Test and at least one math SAT Subject Test (preferably the Math 2 test). Even if you want to be a STEM major, definitely try a few different liberal arts subject tests because those scores can be used to show your breadth of knowledge.

Some colleges such as Georgetown actually require you to submit 3 different SAT Subject Tests. And even if you aren't applying to a school that requires subject tests, many schools say that they are recommended. I personally submitted the SAT US History Subject Test, the SAT Biology Subject Test, and the SAT Math 2 Subject Test to the colleges I applied to. Keep in mind that these subject tests do not replace the full length SAT itself; you still have to take the SAT. But, I think that submitting the extra subject tests gave schools a good idea of the breadth and depth of my ability, so I would highly recommend that all students do the same.

While preparing for specific exams, you should buy the Barron's review book for the specific subject test and also the official College Board book for the specific subject test. The Barron's book will give you material to go over concepts you need to review, and the College Board book will give you official practice tests that you must do. Complete as much practice as possible and go over any material that you don't feel confident about. Here is some specific advice on each of the individual subject tests, which Harvard student, music extraordinaire, and subject test sensei Eric Tarlin generously contributed to:

Science tests	Take these after completing any AP science, and you will be very well prepared. You will only need to learn a few minor things from a review book.
US History/World History	Great to take after AP US History or AP World History because it's very fact-based, and it tests your ability to understand what is going on in different eras
Foreign Languages	A lot of native speakers take these exams, so it's hard to do well, but doing well can be a great way to prove your mastery if you are not a native speaker. And if you are a native speaker, definitely take it and get the 800.

Math 1	This test is really easy and completely useless. Don't take it, but if you do, make sure you 100% get an 800. If you've earned a B or higher in honors precalculus, you should not take this exam. Taking it would be like playing on your high school JV team when you have varsity talent. It's a waste of your time.
Math 2	It would be best to take this test directly after having taken pre-calculus, which gives you all of the knowledge that you need. I recommend taking a few practice tests and brushing up on the types of questions you get wrong. Use Khan Academy or YouTube to help you turn your weakest areas into your sharpest ones. Then pace yourself carefully on the real test and CHECK YOUR WORK for mindless mistakes. Also, make sure that you are able to quickly graph and use other important functions on your calculator, which will help significantly during this test.
English Literature	The best way to prepare for this subject test is to read a lot. After all, this test measures your ability to understand what you're reading. As your exam date approaches, take a practice test or two in order to get used to pacing yourself and to familiarize yourself with the types of questions that you'll encounter. I recommend looking at the questions for each passage before you read so that you know what you're looking for in the text. Go in there fully rested and give it your all!

AP Exams

Consider the AP exams as an opportunity to show your mastery of a subject. Getting a 5 on the national exam (all of which are scored from 1-5) proves that you truly understand the course material.

Exam Timeline

As far as when to take your exams, your timeline should look something like the chart at the end of this chapter. You want to take your SAT Subject Tests soon after your AP exams. If you are a Junior and want to take the full SAT in June, take your Subject Tests in May (at the same time as AP exams). However, if you are not a Junior or have already finished the SAT earlier in the year and have a score that you are happy with, you should take your subject tests in June so that you have a month to take practice tests and prepare.

As far as the SAT, ideally you prepare incredibly hard and only take it once or twice during your Junior year. However, if something goes wrong and you do worse than you did in your practice, you could take it again in the fall of your senior year. Some colleges allow you to superscore (meaning you can submit your best take on each section of the standardized test), so taking the exam more than once can be a good idea. However, if you can take the exam just once and knock it out of the park, that's the ideal situation. Don't go taking the SAT over and over again if you aren't prepared; many colleges are now starting to ask you to send all scores. When you take the exam, prepare seriously, and try not to take it more than three times.

	SAT Subject Tests	AP exams	PSAT/NMSQT	SAT/ACT
Freshman	June			
Sophomore	June	May	Fall	
Junior	May/June	May	Fall	Any months that work well with your personal schedule (varies per person), one or two times
Senior				October (optional)

Section II: Outside the Classroom

Chapter 4

Extracurricular Madness

Don't Be a Jack-of-All-Trades

You need to show colleges that you are passionate about something and talented outside of the classroom. Here's my quick advice for extracurriculars: excel in one area, one specific thing, and put the majority of your focus into it so that it is impressive to the admissions officers and so that you can also be really talented at something for the rest of your life. Maybe it's a sport like football, tennis, golf, or soccer. Or maybe it's an art like theatre, photography, or music. Or maybe it's fixing cars or robotics and programming. Of course, you should supplement your major extracurricular with a few minor extracurriculars that you also truly enjoy to help diversify your intellectual experience, but don't overdo it.

It's much more impressive (and fulfilling) to pursue your interests in your free time than it is to participate in a whole bunch of activities because you think that is what colleges want to see. So don't spread yourself out over eight different extracurriculars. You will probably end up exhausted, stressed, and bad at all of them. Having multiple interests is fantastic, but make sure you're actually committed to the things you spend your time doing. Shallow, uninspired involvement in a laundry list of activities is a waste of your time.

Don't Check the Boxes

Now, I prided myself in my ability to juggle several extracurricular activities while excelling in most of them. But I certainly didn't do as many different things as several students I know did, and if I could do it over again, I would have just focused on what I loved and not tried to "check all the boxes" for the college admissions process.

When you fill out the Common App, you can tell colleges about up to 10 activities you have participated in during all of high school. I found that I had done way more than 10, and that I had really been overextending myself for no reason. Between being a three-season captain and athlete in soccer, track, and tennis, highly involved with my youth group, participating in band and two orchestras, playing in pit orchestra for my school's musicals, singing in choir, and showing up to National Honor Society, I was definitely doing too much. And that's not to mention several of the clubs that I tried. There wasn't even space for me to include the clubs that I participated in (but honestly didn't care too much about) on the Common App. I was just totally wasting my time.

Choosing Activities

Here's what I recommend. I'd break up extracurriculars into four categories: sports, arts, work, and clubs. Obviously there are some things that don't fit in these categories, but for the most part those encompass what you will be choosing to participate in.

During your freshman year, try out ALL of the clubs that you believe might interest you. Even if this means that you need to go to 10 different club meetings, don't be hesitant to try all of them. Talk to members in each club to get a sense of what the club is like, and try out some of the club's standard activities to see if you like it.

No matter how many activities you want to explore, I would also recommend trying out at least one activity in each of the four categories that I mentioned at some point during your high school career (sports, arts, work, and clubs). For example, you could try to play volleyball, participate in the drama company, have a job mowing lawns, and be a part of the robotics club. You should at least *explore* all four categories so that you can expand your horizons and possibly expose yourself to surprising interests.

After you try out many activities during your freshman year, you will begin to find out which ones you are the most passionate about and can make these your major commitments. I can't stress enough that you need to make sure that you *genuinely* enjoy these major commitments. You need to have strong, internal motivation, which is sparked by passion, in order to shine while participating in an activity. You may want to devote the majority of your energy to one major activity (this could be the best way to ensure that you excel on the national and/or international level of this activity), or you could instead attempt to excel in two or even three different major activities. It's all a matter of personal preference, how much effort you want to put into each activity, and where your passions guide you. Of course, you could supplement these activities by participating in a few more interesting, low-commitment clubs, but be very careful not to overextend yourself.

Let me give you a personal example that demonstrates why you should explore many activities and find your passions early on in order to get the most out of your high school career. The only club I ever did that I really enjoyed was the Quiz Bowl Club, which I joined second semester senior year. I did it because I wanted to, not to "check the box" for college admissions, and I loved it! Now, if I had explored more clubs early on in high school and started my involvement with the quiz team much earlier, I would have had my entire high school career to practice and become a very talented player because I really enjoyed the activity. So there is something to be said for trying lots of activities early on in high school to see what you like and then sticking with what you love and eventually becoming a prodigy in that area.

Exploring each of the four categories I suggested above is a great way to show the breadth of your ability, but you also want to show depth and commitment. Remember, one of the activities you participate in needs to be more than just an activity to you. It has to have some meaning to your life and really be a passion of yours.

Founding Your Own Club

This is a possibility that is often overlooked by students, but it can be a very powerful opportunity if you choose to take advantage of it. If there is an academic competition that you would like to participate in (for example, robotics, science competitions, or business competitions) that your school does not have a team for, bring together a group of passionate friends and contact your school administration about starting a club! You may also want to found a club to explore a deep interest that you have and to spread knowledge about this subject to others. Most schools are thrilled by new clubs because they reflect a sense of enthusiasm and a desire to learn amongst the students, so your school will most likely support you. Not only will starting your own club allow you to pursue a passion, but it will also allow you to have an instrumental leadership role in the club. Founding a club can be a great way to show colleges that you are an extremely motivated and confident self-starter.

Why You Need to Get Involved

Do what you love and when you are writing your college essays and explaining your activities, it will be easy to talk about your passion. That's a whole heck of a lot better than trying to explain to a college why you love being a part of a club that you joined because your parents made you. Just make sure you're doing something. Get involved. Don't go home after school and play video games and watch YouTube videos. Get involved with something after school, then do your homework, practice your musical instrument, then maybe play video games and watch YouTube videos (if you have time).

If you excel in one or two extracurricular activities, that's awesome! This will likely open doors for you to take on leadership roles, which will help your decision making, critical thinking, and interpersonal skills. Keep at it, and your activities could make for a great topic for your Common App essay. So figure out what you love and do it.

Follow Your Own Interests, Not the Interests of Others

Colleges don't care too much about what you do as long as you are doing something that you enjoy and that you are excelling while doing it. Don't think that running on the track team looks better than playing on the tennis team, or that Key Club looks better than quiz bowl club. Picking activities based on what somebody else wants (i.e. your parents, friends, or colleges) will not make you happy in the long run, and as a result, you will not succeed in these areas. So you're actually holding yourself back by "doing the right things" like being in a community service club when you'd rather be programming robots, and like being on the swim team even though you hate swimming.

Examples

On the next page, I've categorized a whole bunch of different extracurricular activities that can hopefully give you some ideas of what to try if you are just coming into high school.

Sports	Soccer, golf, baseball, tennis, volleyball, martial arts, track, swimming, football, basketball, frisbee, ping pong, hot yoga, etc.
Arts	Drama company, journalism, photography, painting, band, orchestra, graphic design, choir, marching band, dance, etc.
Work	Lab research, restaurant job, summer camp counselor, tech/business internship, mowing lawns, lifeguard, entrepreneurial ventures, etc.
Clubs	Robotics, Science Olympiad, programming/computer science, National Honor Society, Key Club, quiz bowl team, American Sign Language, Model Congress, Model United Nations, Best Buddies, school paper, etc.

Chapter 5

Your Messy Social Media

Colleges Care About Your Social Media

Most of us post on social media pretty regularly. We post pictures of fun times with friends and dish out great compliments, roasts, and jokes in comment sections. Now, I don't have a problem with you doing any of that. In fact, I do a lot of that myself! But when it comes to the beginning of senior year, it's time to clean out your social media. And I mean a total makeover. Why? Because 35% of colleges look at the social media accounts of students they are considering according to CNN as of 2017 (Wallace, Kelly. "Surprise! Social media can help, not hurt, your college prospects." *CNN*, 10 Feb. 2017, www.cnn.com).

The Solution

Here's my advice: scroll through your profile on every social media account you've ever had and delete, make private, and hide from timeline every post that you think could possibly be questionable. Pretend you are an admissions officer looking through a potential student's social media account. Could a certain post be taken the wrong way if you didn't know an inside joke? DELETE IT! Any sort of political post? DELETE IT! Any post where you say anything negative about anybody or anything else (even jokingly)? DELETE IT! Scroll through everything and delete everything that could be taken the wrong way or leave a bad taste in the admissions committee's mouth.

Potential Positives of Your Social Media

However, there is a flip side to this conversation, which is addressed in the CNN article cited above: you can use your social media account to give yourself an edge over your competitors to get into a top school. If your social media account portrays you as the friendly and passionate individual that you are, it can leave a positive impression on an admissions committee. Your social media accounts don't have to hurt your application. That's why I don't necessarily recommend that students turn all of their social media privacy settings on max during senior year while you're applying for colleges. If everything is private, it might look like you're trying to hide something.

So, instead of making everything private, clean out your social media, and make it advertise yourself. If colleges pull up your social media account and see pictures of you smiling on a hike with friends, hugging your sweet Grandma, hanging out with your family, and volunteering at a local soup kitchen, that could give colleges more reason to accept you. Those sorts of pictures give off a better vibe than everything being blocked and private.

And even if you're not a senior in high school, go clean out your social media anyway. You definitely have a whole lot of embarrassing posts from the 8th grade that you don't remember and that nobody wants to see (including yourself).

In summary, use your social media like it's a supplement to your Common App. Expect colleges to be looking at it. Oh, and that picture you took with your friends at 3:00 AM that you thought was goofy.... yeah that one.... go delete it!

Chapter 6

The Community Service Trend

Community Service is Good

Think beyond yourself. Use your talents and passions for a greater cause. Teach somebody else about your interests. Figure out how you can help other people and take the initiative! Serving your community can be a truly meaningful experience.

Why to Do Community Service

You should do community service to impact aspects of your community that you truly care about, but don't do it if your only reason for serving is to impress college admissions committees. And don't feel like you need to join standard community service organizations like Key Club (although if you enjoy it, do it!). For example, instead of doing service through a common organization, you can run workshops at your community library about subjects that you care about (such as robotics or computer science workshops), or you can offer to mentor young actors and actresses in your local middle school's drama company.

Community Service Is Not Required for College Admissions

Don't get me wrong. Community service is a great thing to do. But do it for the right reasons. <u>Don't do community service expecting it to help you get into a college</u>. And don't do it to check the box in the college admissions process. There is no community service box to check in your college application. I remember many of my friends in high school doing community service regularly, and I was worried that I would have to catch up by doing dozens of hours of volunteer work.

But the fact of the matter is that colleges aren't deciding on prospective students based on how much they volunteer. In fact, there isn't even a section on the Common App where you can write specifically about your community service. Do service if you want to for the benefit of those you are helping, not just specifically for a college admissions edge.

Students who view community service as a college requirement often aren't passionate about it, and they spend their time doing community service activities that they aren't truly invested in. As a result, their college essays about their service come off as shallow because they had no dedication to what they were doing. Only if you have passion for your community service will you then be able to write a superb essay about your experience.

Section III: Putting Together the Application

Chapter 7

Quality College Essays

Jordan Cline, who is a student at Columbia University and employed by their admissions office, says that he truly believes at the end of the day, the personal aspects of an application, like the Common App essays, are what separate the few students who are accepted from the many eligible candidates. An admission officer from Columbia once told him, "Imagine having 10 students with perfect grades, perfect scores, gleaming recommendations, and a laundry list of amazing accomplishments. Your task is to pick statistically less than one of them ... how do you do that?"

Your essays are your chance to stand out and be that "statistically less than one in ten" applicant who will be awarded a spot. They are the place where you can add color and meaning to all the numbers and objective measures. If you have much more personality and genuine interest in a school than most other applicants, that's going to give you a real advantage over other kids with perfect scores.

The purpose of your college personal essay is to showcase strong and unique aspects of your personality to the admissions committee. Members of the committee don't get to personally meet you, so you need to make sure that these essays convey the aspects of your personality that you want them to know about.

Step-By-Step Common App Guide

In order to apply for college, you have to submit an online application through a service such as the Common App or some other application service. You could choose from a wide selection of application services, but I recommend that you use the Common App because it is the most widely accepted by colleges, so you won't have to create as many profiles on other application platforms. Some schools such as the University of California schools, Georgetown, MIT, and a few others either have their own private application service or require a specific one that is not the Common App. However, besides these few exceptions, the advice in this book rests on the assumption that you will be using the Common App for the majority of your applications.

Go to the website commonapp.org and create a profile. Once you have created a profile, you will need to fill out a large amount of personal information. This should be straightforward although you will likely need some information from your parents in several of the sections. You will be asked to report your standardized test scores by typing them into your application, and you will also need to send the official documentation through the College Board.

Personal Essay

The final segment of the general Common App that you will need to fill out is the personal essay. Every year, the prompts change ever so slightly, but the question is always pretty much the same: tell me about yourself in 250-650 words. You can check out the prompts online.

Here's what I recommend: write your Common App essay about yourself, an experience you had that taught you something, a challenge you overcame, or whatever is really interesting and important to you. Think about experiences that illuminate something about your personality and character that you would like to show to colleges. Once you come up with a topic, you can see if it applies to any of the prompts. If your essay topic applies to a prompt, write your essay using that prompt to guide you. If your essay topic doesn't match up with any of the prompts, no worries! The final prompt is always pretty much "write about whatever you feel like"(I'm paraphrasing).

Don't feel confined by any of the prompts like you would if you were in an English class. The prompts can be helpful in giving you ideas and direction, but in the end, colleges want to read about you and what makes you unique. Make sure you actually answer the prompt, but remember, the prompts are mostly just training wheels to get students headed in the right direction.

Starting Your Personal Essay

Ok, now you're sitting in front of a blank word document wondering what to write. Let's talk specifically about how you're going to write this essay. First, start with something exciting, interesting, or strange that will catch the college admissions committee's attention immediately. Some ideas for that include:

- Starting with dialogue. For example, a conversation that changed your life or words that you or somebody else shouted before or while something extraordinary was happening in your life.

- A quotation from someone famous (but be careful not to be cliche)

- A strange statistic or piece of trivia that relates to the rest of your essay

- A play-by-play anecdote (short story) of a past event (maybe from your childhood)

- Imagery
- Expression of emotions in a moment

Here's how I started my Common App essay. Note how I used a memory with imagery and emotion to catch the reader's attention:

"I brushed my teeth, put on my Winnie the Pooh footie pajamas, and curled up on the family room sofa with the aroma of dinner lingering in the air. I opened up my book and began to read. I laughed along with the centaurs at Rabadash the Ridiculous and cried with the old Kings and Queens of Narnia as the world ended. Everything felt right in the world. I was safe, and I was smiling."

I used this memory in order to lead into a discussion about my lifelong quest for knowledge outside of the classroom through books (and also ultimately through the internet, podcasts, and great conversations).

The Body of Your Essay

Now you need to tie your opening hook into the body of your essay where you will ideally allow the admissions committee to begin to see who you are. Ideas for what you could lead into a discussion about include:

- How you overcame a challenge. This could be a personal challenge or something in sports/music/drama/etc.
- Your first time doing something (stepping outside your comfort zone)
- How you developed a passion or interest you have (the more unique the better)
- Anything impressive that you have done that makes you unique
- An interaction with someone that illuminates positive character traits or improvement
- A time when you grew/matured
- The importance of your heritage/nationality
- Anything else (don't feel confined by these suggestions) as long as it shows positive personal qualities

Topics that you do NOT want to talk about because they are overly cliché or simply a very bad idea include:

- Don't write about your service/missions trip. I'm sure going on a service trip is something you feel passionate about and want to write about, but believe me, five hundred thousand other students are going to write that exact same essay as you, so it won't make you unique. Plus, writing an essay like that is really just you tooting your own horn saying, "look how nice of a person I am." Further, that sort of an essay fails to give the college admissions committee an accurate picture of who you really are.

- Don't write an essay that praises somebody else who is your role model. Remember this essay is about you, not your sweet Aunt Ruth.

- Don't copy your essay or even small portions of your essay from somewhere else. Every year, kids from high schools (including mine) do this. And every year they get caught. Bad idea.

- Don't write the "I'm a Christian/ Jewish/ Muslim/ atheist/etc" essay. I personally am a devout Christian, and there were places in my application where I talked about how certain elements of my faith affect my choices, but your college admissions essay is neither the time nor the place for you to write a sermon. No college admissions officer wants to read an essay where you quote John 3:16 and your life verse to them for 650 words. You aren't telling them anything that they don't already know, and there are also a whole lot of students who will write this exact essay. Don't be like them. Be more you unique. My only exception to this would be if you are applying to religious colleges, in which case that sort of an essay could be appropriate or even advantageous.

- Don't write shopping list paragraphs where you list things you have done. You'll know you're doing it wrong if you are writing words like "first" or "secondly" or "finally". Your essay should not be a regurgitation of your résumé or activities list (which colleges will be able to see elsewhere). Your essay should be entirely different than the other elements of your application and mainly anecdotal. Make sure this essay tells a story that shows your personality in a way that your résumé and activities list can't.

- Don't write a political rant for your essay. Remember that everyone has biases, and if the person reading your essay has a bias against your viewpoint, don't expect to get accepted.

When to Write Your Personal Essay

You are going to want to start working on your Common App essay during the summer before your senior year because you will have more time to think and brainstorm with less pressure than during the school year. You must continue to work on it through the beginning of your senior year; however, once your senior year starts you will be swamped with dozens of supplemental college essays. The supplemental essay prompts get released much later than the Common App personal essay prompts, so make sure you have your Common App personal essay squared away before the start of senior year and completely finalized by October so that you have more room to breathe during senior fall.

The Three Writing Stages

While writing the essay, keep in mind that you should first outline your idea for the essay and talk it over with multiple people in what I'd call the "carpenter phase". You want a solid framework from which you will build a cohesive essay. Then, write a rough draft in what I'd call the "madman phase" where you just write like crazy. Use your framework to guide you, but write without thinking too much. Don't worry about typos or grammar errors. Get your ideas down on paper so you have a complete product to work with. After the rough draft is done, give the essay some space for a few days. When you come back to the essay, make any necessary major modifications to the structure, and at this point start getting input from other folks as you slowly hone your essay down into a piece of refined literary precious metal in what I'd call the "silversmith phase". This final phase could last a month as you shave your essay down into something truly special.

Editing Your Personal Essay

This essay is going to be submitted to every college you apply to, so it needs to be perfect. You should spend five times as much effort and time on this essay as on any other essay you've written in the past. Write draft after draft after draft after draft after draft after draft. Edit, shave off excess, and add literary devices, metaphors, and clever wordplay. This needs to be the best writing you have ever done.

Have the essay read and edited by family members, college students, and teachers. Take criticism from people you trust. It's hard, but it's helpful. However, also understand that in the end this is your essay and you don't need to take every piece of advice that people give you. You need to strike a balance between taking feedback and making sure that the essay reflects your own voice. If you apply too much external advice, your essay may not show your personality the way you want it to.

When taking advice, a good strategy to use is to look over each piece of advice and make sure you understand why the person suggested it. If you don't understand, clarify it with them. Then, use your judgement to see if their reasoning makes sense and to make sure that their suggestion doesn't take away from the message of your essay. I know from personal experience that some suggestions people gave me for my essay were not good suggestions, so you can't just take their comments as gospel. But if multiple people highlight a similar issue, you know they are onto a legitimate problem with your essay.

Selling Yourself

You want your essay to sell yourself as a product, but in no way whatsoever should you go over your résumé like a shopping list in this essay. Use a story to expound upon your perseverance, diligence, integrity, exceptional intellectual curiosity, ability to grow, and application of criticism. Sell yourself through a compelling narrative. You have to brag about yourself quite subtly. It's a bit of an art, and that's why it will take the editing of a lot of other folks in order to strike the right balance. Ultimately, you want your entire application to be similar to a legal justification building the case for why you should be admitted. To do this, your essay should focus specifically on being a lens that reveals the positive aspects of your personality and how you are an individual of honorable character. The only other chance you have to do this is in your interview.

Be Yourself in Your Writing

It's best to present your true self in these essays. Real people are reading thousands of applications, and they don't want to hear things you think they want to hear; they want to get to know the real you. And when you're presenting your genuine self, your application all makes sense. A great application connects all the dots. There are candidates who can successfully create an artificial narrative, but many of us can't. So it's best to be safe and just be yourself. Talk about what you actually like to do and what interests you. However, this doesn't mean that you shouldn't spend much time to drafting these essays in thoughtful ways.

Don't Make Stupid Mistakes

Small typos and blatant errors point to poor proofreading and can almost immediately remove you from the selective applicant pools. When you're crafting your narrative about yourself, an error demonstrates you don't care enough about yourself and your presentation to the world. Thus, you must edit incredibly carefully. Keep in mind that your brain will sometimes gloss over your own errors; that's why you need other people to read through your essays.

Personal Essay Length

You want your personal essay word count to be over 600 but obviously less than the 650 maximum. If your word count is any shorter than 600, the essay will look short and you will look lazy. If your essay is only 540 words long, you are missing out on the opportunity to give the admissions committee 110 more words that justify why you should be accepted.

Reading Other People's Personal Essays

If you want a model for a decent Common App essay, go online or talk to college students and read successful Common App essays. Many different approaches and styles have been successful. So be creative! Hopefully, reading other essays will give you some inspiration and nudge you in the right direction. Just be sure not to read too other many essays to the point where you base your essay off of somebody else's. You want yours to be completely unique. Remember, everybody else's essays are going to look exactly like the online samples. You need to be different.

Supplemental Essays

Most colleges you apply to will ask for somewhere around 2 to 4 supplemental "essays" (using the word "essay" loosely as most of these "essays" are hardly a small paragraph in length). These supplemental essays are short responses to very specific questions such as "tell me about an extracurricular activity you participated in" or "why do you want to go to this university?" or "tell me about your community/friend group" or "what excites you about learning?". Sometimes these supplements are abstract, such as for the University of Chicago, while others are very precise. But in the end, all of your responses need to be specific to each school because the schools are asking why you want to go to *their* school and why you want to be in one of *their* specific programs. Even if a supplement prompt sounds general, it is meant specifically for their school or program.

Some colleges don't require any supplements, but instead have an optional supplemental essay. You must do every optional essay. Think about what message you are sending if you don't do the optional essay. You are literally telling the college "I don't care enough to put in the effort to write this essay." So don't be surprised when you get rejected if you don't do the optional supplemental essay(s).

Your Supplement Strategy

You should write around five high-quality supplemental essays for the first few colleges you apply to (presumably the colleges you apply to early action/ decision). These short answer responses will act as a template for the supplemental essays you will write for the remaining colleges you plan to apply to. In other words, if you are applying to 10 schools, you shouldn't write 35 entirely unique supplemental essays. You can use the same essays over and over again, just carefully craft them to fit each question. Make sure the details of the essay are very specific to each school you apply to, but you can keep the structure the same and reuse material about yourself.

Answering Why You Want to Go to a Certain College

For example, most colleges ask for a short essay on why you want to go to their school. Write a quality essay about how it has a specific degree/program you want, quality professors, a vibrant community, perfect location, specific classes, clubs, labs, opportunities, etc. Then for the next college you apply to, use the same structure, but tweak it to personalize it to the specific college. You will have to be very careful in doing this because you want your essays to be as specific as possible, but this can be a way to save a lot of time if you are applying to 10+ schools. Make sure you use specific names of programs, colleges, the university, extracurriculars, and anything else you are interested in. If you are too vague, it will be obvious that you are copying and pasting a generic template.

Answering What Your Passion Is

As another example, let's say you have a great essay you wrote about how much you love playing violin and how it taught you to work hard and how it means the world to you and how you named your violin and how you want to continue playing in an orchestra in college. So let's say you wrote this essay for a college that asked you, "what is your passion?". This essay works perfectly! But let's say another college asks you, "what's something you want to continue doing in college?". Bingo! Use the same essay! Let's say there is another college that asks you, "what is an extracurricular that taught you something?". Once again, the same essay works. Even for an essay that asks, "what's unique about you?", you could perfectly well use the same essay again by explaining how you were the only kid to name your violin! See how this works? Obviously, you will need to do some shuffling of the essays and changing word counts here and there, but this will save you a lot of time.

Answering Why You Chose Your Area of Interest

Another common question is "why are you drawn to the area(s) of study you indicated earlier in this application?" Make sure you don't say generic things like, "I want to use a Computer Science education to innovate technology that changes the world". It's a trap that students fall into, and these general responses are not specific to you and literally say nothing unique about you! Make sure that you mention specific topics that interest you and what you would like to accomplish. For example, you could mention how you want to use computer science and engineering to improve athletic training, recovery, and data analytics in sports because you have interests in tech and sports. That's so much better than vaguely saying, "I want to change the world".

Abstract Prompts

Many schools such as Stanford, Columbia, and University of Chicago, have supplemental prompts that are quite abstract and unconventional. Feel free to look specifically at Columbia's book list, Stanford's roommate prompt, and all of University Chicago's supplements for abstract essay examples. Remember that you should not simply answer the questions. Rather, frame your answers in such a way that you send the message about who you are as a person that you want to send to that specific school. Be really creative with these and be willing to take risks. You aren't going to get in if you play these prompts conservatively. BE BOLD!

Chapter 8

Letters of Recommendation

Be a good, genuine person. Teacher recommendation letters play a significant role in the admissions process at most colleges, so don't be an idiot in the classroom. You will need at least two letters of recommendations from teachers and one more letter from your guidance counselor for a total of three letters of recommendation.

Communicate with Your Guidance Counselor

Your guidance counselor knows he or she has to write you a recommendation letter, so they will be expecting you to make an appointment and fill out a form in which you tell them everything about yourself that they don't already know. Then, your counselor will write you a letter, and you're all set! Easy.

Try to get to know your guidance counselor more than other students. Meet with him or her a few times each year to talk about classes and ask for high school advice, about summer opportunities, and about what you can do during your early high school years to be on the right track to getting into a top school. The better they get to know you and your interests, the better your letter of recommendation will be. If you visit them for advice, they will also see that you are a curious and driven student, which can be reflected in your recommendation letter. It is sometimes hard to do this, especially at big schools, but if you can, really make an effort to talk even just while passing in the halls. It will give you a more personal guidance recommendation—something that many people don't have— which can give you the upper hand over your competition.

When to Ask for Teacher Recommendations

When it comes to teacher recs, things get a little trickier. You are going to want to ask two teachers for letters at the end of your junior year so that they can have time to write their letters over the summer before the fall of your senior year. If you aren't able to or forget to ask your teachers during your junior year, you can ask at the beginning of senior year. However, keep in mind that this might cause them to rush your letter or potentially turn you down because the teacher you want has already been asked by so many people. So just don't do this. It's stupid, and it shows the teachers that you didn't think ahead. If you can be one of the first people to ask a teacher for a letter of recommendation, they will be more likely to say yes and more likely to do a great job.

Which Teachers to Ask

As far as who to ask, since you are asking at the end of your junior year, you will most likely want teachers from junior year that you have great relationships with. If you don't have great relationships with two teachers from junior year, you could ask a teacher from sophomore year; however, chances are they don't remember you as well. And I wouldn't even consider asking a teacher from freshman year because they can't really give an accurate representation of who you are as a senior. You could always take a gamble and ask a teacher from senior year. But, you will have to ask them in the first few weeks of the fall of your senior year, which means that you will have very little time to get to know your teachers, so I would not recommend this. Obviously, don't pick a teacher that you didn't ever take a class with.

It's best to pick teachers from classes that you were legitimately interested in and did really well in. Make sure the teacher thinks highly of you. If this teacher is also your club advisor or coach, that could make for a really strong recommendation. If you want to get into a top-tier school, you often need recommendations that say that "this student was the most motivated/strongest student that I taught this year or ever had" (or something of the sort). Even if you can't get that strong of a recommendation, make sure that the teacher can speak highly of your intellect, curiosity, perseverance, and personality.

If possible, ask teachers from different subject areas. If you could ask one humanities teacher and one science/math teacher, that would be a perfect scenario. I asked an English teacher, who I had been both a student and a TA for, as well as my biology teacher, who I had a great relationship with. Pairing different subject areas is a great way to show that you work hard regardless of the academic discipline. If you could ask a math and history teacher, that would be awesome! Or if you asked a language teacher and physics teacher, that's perfect! What you don't want is the band teacher and the choir teacher; or your two favorite English teachers; or your two favorite math teachers; or an English teacher and a history teacher; or even a math teacher and a biology teacher. Diversity in subject area is key here. So pick the one math/science teacher and the one humanities teacher who will speak the most highly of you.

What to Give Your Teachers When You Ask for a Rec

When you ask a teacher for a letter of recommendation, you should give them one of those large yellow mail envelopes, and put your résumé, transcript, and test scores inside. Type out specific examples of ways you showed your character or intelligence in the teacher's classroom and put the sheet of paper in the envelope as well. Write your name, your teacher's name, and the date you need the letter submitted by on the outside of the envelope. This makes it easy for your teacher because all the materials are in one place. Also, your teacher will be less likely to lose or forget about your letter. Some teachers give you the opportunity to talk to them about what you want them to highlight in their letter of recommendation, so make sure to do this if they offer. Think of ways that you stood out in their class and be prepared to talk about specific examples, but be sure to also give them the envelope with your written materials.

Additional Letters of Recommendation

Beyond teacher recommendations, consider the fact that many of your coaches, club advisors, and mentors may know you better than your teachers, and they are perfectly eligible to write you additional letters of recommendation. They could give the college admissions committees a great perspective on a different side of you. Most colleges allow you to upload up to two more recommendations (in addition to your two teacher recommendations) from employers, private instructors, coaches, club advisors, clergy, mentors, friends, and family. If you interned or worked somewhere and had a great experience, your employer or anybody you had a close relationship with at your workplace could write a great letter on your work ethic and intelligence in the real world. Personally, I asked my youth pastor from my church and my French horn teacher to write additional letters of recommendation for me. I think that their added perspectives were particularly influential in my acceptance into universities.

Chapter 9

Detailing Your Activities

Strong applicants obviously spend lots of time outside of school participating in activities that they are passionate about. However, taking part in the activities is only the start of a student's journey towards a successful college application. Effectively describing your extracurricular activities and highlighting your specific roles in these activities is a crucial yet often overlooked aspect of college applications. This chapter will discuss the two key places in which you will need to do this: the Common App activities list and personal résumé.

Common App Activities

Good news folks—activities lists are not hard! This is the part of the show where you finally get to write that shopping list of all your accomplishments, awards, and hard work over the years.

While filling out the Common App, you will be asked to detail 10 activities that you participated in during high school. This may seem pretty simple, but you need to pack as much detail into as few words as possible in this section because your word count is strictly limited. Don't take this section lightly. Be sure to fill out all 10 of the activities. You will have definitely participated in more than 10 things in high school by the time you graduate, so really rack your brain to think of great ideas.

You DON'T want to use complete sentences while describing your activities, but rather you want to cram in as much detail as possible about your accomplishments in each extracurricular activity. There is a strict 150 character limit in your description of each activity, so highlight as much as possible using commas and short phrases. For example, if you did track in high school, under the activity name section, say "Hurdler and Jumper, Varsity Captain, Springfield High School". Under the description of this activity and what you accomplished say, "Captain 2 years. Varsity letter 4 years. State relay meet and state decathlon all 4 years. Taught incoming freshman how to hurdle." See how much info is packed into just a few words? Also note how personal accomplishments and leadership roles (captain, teaching freshmen), not just general team descriptions, are featured in the description. Do the same for all your activities!

Order your activities from the most impressive and important to least impressive and important. It's always better to highlight your biggest accomplishments first. Be sure to highlight YOUR specific role/impact in each activity, not just a general description of what the activity is. For example, if you participated on a robotics team, don't just list the general objective of the team. Instead, you could state that you were the "lead programmer" on the team and could go on to list any awards/accomplishments.

Listing Your Honors

You will also have space to list five honors on your application. Choose these awards wisely (you don't want to be listing a recreational basketball sportsmanship award as 20% of your awards section). Jokes aside, select the five most prestigious honors that you have obtained. Additionally, in order to use your limited space wisely, list awards that are related to extracurriculars in the activities section of your application, NOT in the honors section. For example, personal music awards (county, district, all-state, and regional band/orchestra), sports achievements, quiz bowl championships, and robotics awards can all go under their respective activities in the activities list, so they shouldn't go in the honors section. Personal awards that are not related to any of these activities can then be included in the honors section.

Utilizing Extra Space in Your Application

The application also has space for you to write anything that you didn't include in other parts of the application. ABSOLUTELY take advantage of this space. Not only will it allow you to list any activities or important awards that you did not list in previous sections, but it will also allow you to write a couple of extra sentences about your accomplishments in an activity that you may have not been able to fit in the activities section.

Keep in mind that this is not space for you to rant about every single one of your activities. Only list material here if you think it will add significant value to your application. For example, you can write two sentences each about your role in two different activities that you had not listed elsewhere, or list more awards related to an activity that you could not fit in the activities section.

Crafting Your Résumé

Many colleges allow you to submit a résumé, and chances are that when you apply for summer jobs, you will have to write a résumé, so you will need to polish up any current résumé you have or create a new one.

Résumé Size

If you can fit your résumé on one page, that would be ideal. Definitely do not go over two full pages. Better to highlight just a few big accomplishments than to rapid-fire 50 pretty meh participation awards you got over the years.

Résumé Organization

You want your résumé to look clean, so make sure that you are using bulleted lists organized with nice titles and subtitles. You should definitely list your school, hometown, GPA, and relevant standardized test scores near the top.

You can divide your résumé into significant sections - Academics/Awards, Work/Intern Experience, Leadership and Activities, and Volunteer Work. Under each category, list relevant items and dates.

For one-time awards, you can list the award and year in which the award was achieved, as well as a brief description (if necessary):

Won town-wide essay competition (2016)

For activities, which you participated in over multiple years and which require more detailed descriptions, include the starting and ending years as well as more information. Let's say you were part of the computer science club from 2014-2017 and were the president of the club for your last 2 years:

Computer Science Club (2014 - 2017):
· President (2016-2017)
· Organized club meetings and events at high school to foster interest in programming

There are many ways to organize résumés, so ask your parents, relatives, and friends if you can take a look at their résumés for inspiration. You can also consult Google for example résumés, and many colleges have résumé advice on their office of career services department websites, which may be helpful.

Starting Early

I'd recommend starting to plan the process of creating an activities list, awards list, and résumé very early. If you are an underclassman in high school, whenever you get an award or start a new activity, write it down in a doc called "college résumé" or something of the sort, and include a brief description. Believe me, when senior year rolls around, you won't remember much from the younger years, so it's helpful to have an index of your accomplishments for the activities list, awards section, and résumé. Also, making a résumé before senior year can help you get ahead of the game for any job or internship opportunities. I would strongly recommend making your résumé near the end of sophomore year.

Chapter 10

How Many Applications?

There are a number of factors that come into play when considering how many colleges you should apply to. At a bare minimum, you should apply to 8 colleges. Anything less would be risky and ill-advised. You want to apply to at least 2 safety schools, at least 4 target schools, and as many reach schools as you have time and money to apply for.

My College Application List and Results

Figuring out a good breakdown for yourself is important. I applied to 12 colleges, and I think that anywhere between 10 and 16 colleges is probably a safe range to be in. Out of the 12 colleges I applied to, I was accepted into five:

University of Michigan, University of Notre Dame, Vanderbilt University, University of Rochester, and Wheaton College. And I ended up deciding to go to Vandy! Anchor Down!!!

Cast a Wide Net of Applications

Here's what you need to take away from this: there are schools that you may think you will definitely get into that will reject you, but there will also be schools that you think you have no chance at that will accept you. So cast a wide net. Every extra school you apply to is like giving yourself an extra die in a game of chance where if you roll a one, you get in. If you only have one die, your chances aren't good, but if you have 12 dice, you will most likely roll a few ones and get into several places. Obviously the game of college admissions isn't entirely chance, but you see what I'm getting at.

Getting into several different schools also puts you in a position where you can choose the best financial aid package and have some leverage with the college that you want to go to. If you only apply to four schools, you will probably only get into one and then be forced to go there even if they don't give you great scholarships and grants.

Picking Safeties

In order to pick your safety schools, consider a few things. First, you need to pick safety schools that you would be happy to go to. Yes, going to a safety school is less than ideal, but there are a lot of options for safeties. So pick ones that you know you would be happy with—they could have decent overall academics, or just a strong program in the major that you are interested in.

Also, whatever college your parents (or a parent) went to is probably a safety school for you (as long as it isn't a school like Harvard). Universities generally love to accept legacy students, so you may have a higher probability of acceptance at a parent's school. Further, many colleges have special scholarships for alumni children who are accepted, so you will most likely get a great financial aid package. My parents both went to University of Rochester, so for me it was a safety school.

Another great option for a safety school is your flagship state university. Whether it is the University of Massachusetts, Ohio State, or Penn State, applying to your state school can be a great idea because that school will give you cheap in-state tuition and will also give you priority for admissions as an in-state resident. You could also consider other state schools in your state that might not be as highly ranked but have a great program in the subject that you want to study (i.e. University of Massachusetts Lowell has a quality engineering program).

Another option for a safety school is a small liberal arts college with a high acceptance rate. There are a number of small liberal arts colleges across the country with beautiful campuses that offer quality education.

Also, when looking at safety schools, a good measure is seeing where your SAT/ACT score falls on their spectrum. Most schools report their 25 percentile and 75th percentile scores. Having a standardized test score that is greater than a school's 75th percentile is usually a pretty good indication that the school is a safety school. An exception to this rule is if you have a near perfect SAT score and your score is greater than the 75th percentile for Ivies and schools like Vandy and Duke. Trust me, those are not safety schools. So take this 75th percentile rule with a grain of salt.

Picking Targets

For target schools, it's always a good idea to have a large selection of great schools that have average GPAs and test scores similar to your own. Definitely include several large state universities that have great reputations such as University of Virginia, University of Michigan, and UCLA. And of course you should also apply to some more competitive liberal arts colleges that you are personally interested in such as Notre Dame, Lehigh, and Northeastern. Everybody's target schools will be different. For some people, target schools will have acceptance rates around 60% while for others it will be closer to 25%. But don't let your target schools creep much lower than 25% acceptance rates even if you are a top student.

Every year there are students who think that Ivy League schools (plus Stanford, MIT, Caltech, and the like) are their target schools, and then they don't get into any of the top schools which they applied to. In this case, they may be stuck going to safety schools that they didn't put much thought into. You will most likely end up going to one of your target schools, so you should pick schools which you would actually want to go to and you can realistically get into.

Taking Your Shot at Reach Schools

Although your acceptance to a reach school is far from guaranteed, you should still try. This is your one chance to apply as an undergraduate, so take it. Even if you are not a straight-A student with a 1550+ SAT score, apply to at least a few reach schools. However, if you are at the top of your class and have strong test scores and extracurriculars, I would apply to as many top tier schools as possible (8+). Here's why: the admissions process for Ivy League level schools is very complex and involves many different factors. There are so many qualified applicants who apply that many of them have to be rejected. If you apply to 8+ top schools, and you are qualified, you can hedge your bets that you will get into at least one. Go for it!

Application Costs

Keep in mind that each application will cost you about $100 (by the time you include the cost of sending scores and supplements) and probably a minimum of eight solid hours of work, so only apply if you really want to go to the school. If you start doing your applications early enough in senior fall, you will have plenty of time to do as many Ivy League applications as you want, but don't put yourself in a position where those are the only schools you apply to not matter how smart you are.

How to Decide on Your Short List of 10-16 Colleges

Here are some factors to consider when you are picking which schools to apply to and ultimately which one you will attend:

Strength of Specific Departments

Pick schools with strong academic programs and departments in the subject(s) that you are interested in. For example, MIT is known for computer science and engineering; if you want to be a journalist, MIT will not necessarily be on your shortlist. Many schools have strong programs across the board, but if you dig deep enough, you will find that they have certain programs that really stand out.

Academic Structure

There are colleges that have strict academic requirements and force students to take classes across all disciplines, colleges that have absolutely no class requirements, and colleges that fall somewhere in between. Just because colleges are ranked highly does not mean that they have similar academic structure. The colleges in the top tier all have different class requirements, so visit their websites in order to explore these requirements and decide which ones best suit your preferences. Do you want to go to a school that gives you lots of academic freedom, which you could use to explore many unique fields or focus specifically on certain subjects? Would you like a school that ensures that you and all other students will explore various academic disciplines together? Or do you not really have a preference? These are important questions to consider when assessing academic structure.

Special Programs

Certain universities also have specific programs that combine different subjects. For example, this could be Biology and Computer Science or Business and Biomedical Engineering. Look for these specific programs if you are passionate about the intersection of multiple fields! Additionally, if you are interested in music, music schools often partner with other colleges to offer programs that allow you to obtain a degree from both a music school and another college.

Location

Obviously, this isn't the most important concern because, as best as I can tell, most 17-year-olds don't really know whether or not they fully like or dislike certain locations because their experience is limited... anyhow... rant aside, things like how much money you get in scholarships will probably take precedence over location, but it's worth considering.

For some students, closeness to home is important. If this matters to you, try to apply to more local schools. However, please don't limit yourself too much by only applying to nearby schools because there could be great fits for you that are just a few states away.

Culture

Some schools are strictly academically focused while others are total zoos (lit party schools), but most fall somewhere in the middle of that spectrum. It's important to find a school that has a work/life balance that suits your personality. You'll want the school to have the sorts of extracurriculars you are genuinely interested in and a certain level of academic rigor that you can handle.

If you are into entrepreneurship, you should look for schools that are known for their entrepreneurial culture. College is one of those rare times in life during which you will be surrounded by intelligent people with a diverse skill set. This is the perfect environment for you to put together a startup.

Talking to Those With Experience

Talk to alumni and current students about the school that you want to go to. If the school is within driving distance (or if you are willing to fly), visiting is really helpful. Ask as many questions as you can when you are there. Go on the general campus tour, but also explore on your own and go on a department-specific tour if one is available in your area of interest (like an engineering tour).

Quick Hack to Increase Admissions Chances

Find out which colleges your high school is known for sending students to. For example, if your school sends 10 students every year to University of Rochester, then applying to University of Rochester is definitely a great decision. Universities tend to have favorite high schools that they pick top students from (known as feeder schools). Sometimes your high school has students regularly go to a few top-tier schools. Play the odds to your advantage by applying to colleges where your high school has a good reputation.

Keep Everything in Perspective

When you finally hear back from all the schools that you are applying to, set aside your ego. Most students can thrive at most schools. A rejection does not mean that you are not qualified, it just means that the admissions committee didn't think you were the best fit for their incoming class. Luckily, colleges are more similar across the board than most people think; academically, you get out what you put in. Chances are you will find wonderful friends and awesome extracurricular activities wherever you end up!

Here's some more good news: you might not have to do all these applications if you get into your favorite school early action or early decision. I'll explain more about how to apply early and why you should apply early in the next chapter.

Chapter 11

Regular Decision vs. Early Action/Decision

There's a lot of confusion about the different deadlines that colleges offer for applications. Let's start by defining our terms.

Regular Decision (RD)

Applications are due around January 1 . You will generally hear back around April 1.

Early Action (EA)

Applications are due around November 1. You will probably hear back in late December.

Restrictive Early Action (REA)

Harvard, Yale, Princeton, and Stanford (HYPS) all use this special form of Early Action. If you apply to any of these schools restrictive EA, you aren't forced to attend if you get in. However, if you apply restrictive EA, you can't apply early action or early decision to any other private institutions. So if you apply restrictive EA to one of HYPS, you could also apply EA to other state universities but not any private institutions. Applications are due around November 1. You will generally hear back in late December.

Early Decision (ED)

This is a binding contract that states that if you get into the college, you must enroll in the college, so you can only apply early decision to one school. Applications are due around November 1. You will generally hear back in late December.

Rolling Admissions

Some schools have rolling admissions and allow you to apply pretty much whenever. You will generally hear back in a few weeks. These schools are usually not particularly competitive, but they could be good options for safety schools.

Why You Must Apply Early

The majority of your applications will be regular decision. However, you have the opportunity to apply to at least one school early, and you should certainly take advantage of it. Most schools have a much higher acceptance rate for early action and early decision applicants. Even better, if you are deferred during the early phase, your application will get considered again in the regular decision phase. So applying early gives you two tries and better chances on your first try.

If there is one school with an ED option that is a bit of a reach school for you, but you are 100% confident that you want to go there, you should apply early decision to take advantage of the boost in acceptance rate. Colleges want to accept as many early decision students as possible because this will increase their yield (the number of accepted students who enroll). Colleges want students they accept to actually attend the school. If students are accepted and don't attend, it makes the college look bad and thus go down in rankings. So, because all early decision admits are required to attend by contract, schools love accepting students early decision.

Don't lock yourself into a mediocre school by applying early decision to a school that isn't the best you could do. Sometimes students run into problems where they get in early decision and are locked into going to a school, but the school did not offer enough financial aid or isn't the best fit for them. You don't want that to be you.

Using Your EA/ED Wildcard Wisely

Think of your early decision application as your wildcard boost for a reach school. There are basically two strategies that a student can take regarding applying early action or early decision (EA/ED). The first one is applying to your dream school no matter how hard it is to get in. This school could be among the hardest schools to get into: Harvard, Stanford, MIT, Princeton, Yale, etc. Whichever it is, if you love it the most, if you know you have the profile to possibly get in, just apply EA/ED because you want to maximize your chances of getting into the college of your dreams.

The second strategy is to apply EA/ED to a top tier-school that has a slightly less absurdly low acceptance rate: schools like Georgetown, UVA, Carnegie Mellon, USC, UCLA, Notre Dame, Brown, Dartmouth, UPenn, Cornell, Duke, Vanderbilt, Northwestern, etc. The top applicants around the country are generally applying EA/ED to the likes of Harvard, Stanford, and Yale, so if you apply to schools just one tier below, you may not have to face as many top applicants (although the applicant pool will obviously still be incredibly challenging). Your best shot at getting into a great school is probably applying ED to a school in that second tier range (Duke, Vandy, Brown, etc.). But remember, if you get in ED, you have to go, and you can't apply anywhere else. So if you really love one of these "one step below Harvard" schools, apply to it EA/ED instead of one of the ultra competitive top 5 schools. However, if you dream of going to Harvard or Stanford or an equivalent school, and you have the profile to get in, you should apply to your dream school because you don't want to deprive yourself of this once-in-a-lifetime opportunity.

Applying early decision or restrictive early action is a bold move, but by looking at the chart below, you can see why so many students opt to give it a shot:

2018 Acceptance Rates

School	Restrictive Early Action/ Early Decision Acceptance Rate	Overall Acceptance Rate
Harvard University (REA)	14.5%	4.6%
Duke University (ED)	21.4%	8.3%
University of Pennsylvania (ED)	18.5%	8.4%
Vanderbilt University (ED)	20.5%	10.7%
Princeton University (REA)	14.7%	5.5%
Yale University (REA)	14.36%	6.3%

As you can see from the chart, at a number of these universities, your chances of being accepted early are around twice your chances of being accepted regular decision. And keep in mind that the "Overall Acceptance Rate" is a combination of the regular decision and early action/decision rate. So, at most of these schools, the true regular decision acceptance rate is much lower than the written "Overall Acceptance Rate".

Early Scholarships

Some schools have special scholarship deadlines that are much earlier (for example, in December) than the normal RD deadline. If you would like to be considered for these scholarships, you would have to submit your regular decision application early enough for this special deadline or apply EA/ED.

Don't Wait to Start Your RD Applications

Caution: If you apply EA or ED, DON'T wait for your early results to come out before you start working on your regular decision applications. This is one of the biggest mistakes that students make. Most EA/ED results come out around December 15, and regular decision applications are due around January 1. Half a month is not even close to enough time for you to write, edit, and perfect supplemental essays for 10+ colleges. Also, December break starts around December 23th in most places. If you are starting regular apps on the 15th, that gives you very few days to contact your school/guidance office for anything that you need. Again, not enough time. Before your EA/ED material is due, work as hard as you can on it. Once you hit submit, work on your regular decision applications like you aren't going to get into any of your EA/ED schools. Try to finish several drafts of your RD applications and get some feedback by the normal EA/ED result time (Dec 15). If you get into your reach school early, awesome! If not, you are in good position to perfect and submit your regular decision applications. Also, make sure that you get everything that you need from your high school (transcripts, teacher recommendations, and teacher feedback on essays) well before December break begins. You won't get any help from your school during December break, and when you get back from break, it will be too late.

Chapter 12

Perfecting Your Interviews

Interviews may seem scary, but don't stress about them. An alumnus from the university you are applying to will conduct the interview. This means that most of the interviewers are very approachable and will tell you a lot about the school. The alumni who conduct the interviews don't have too much sway over your admissions decision. So relax, demonstrate your passion, and be your charming self in the interview process. You will be fine!

The Interview Play-By-Play

Here's how the interviews work. An interviewer generally emails you saying that they've been assigned to interview you. Sometimes you have to reach out to them, but that is a much rarer case. When replying to their email, be respectful with a proper greeting (Dear Mr./Ms./Dr.) and closing (Sincerely, Regards, Thanks,). Before you meet with the interviewer, it's not a bad idea to briefly research them. Don't be creepy and stalk them, but you can do things like finding out what their profession is with simple google searches. Obviously, don't walk into your interview and say, "so you work for Google huh...". But keep what you know about them in your mind as you enter the interview because it will give you a better idea of how to approach the person and the conversation topics that you could connect on.

Once you've set up a time and location via email, you will show up at a local library or coffee shop and have a casual conversation with your interviewer about the school that you hope to attend. During the interview, find ways to weave in conversation topics that you are passionate about and would love to talk about. This could be technology, history, or non-academic topics like art and sports. For example, if you like sports and you get an opportunity to talk about what you did last night or do in your free time, you can slide in, "I was watching the Celtics game last night. Watching basketball is one of my favorite things to do." And then before you know it, you're talking sports, and your interviewer gets to see you talk about something you're passionate about. Be casual about this; it's a hard thing to do, but if you are good in conversation and confident, try it. If they like the topic as well, you could get into a good conversation and connect well. If they don't expand on it, you can just talk about whatever their next topic is and move with the flow of the interview and probably drone on about why you want to go to their university.

Once the interview is over, the alumnus will write a report to the admissions office about the interview. The report will go in a pile with all of your other application materials: letters of recommendation, essays, test scores, and personal information. The content in the interviewer's letter will hold about as much weight as one of your teacher's letters of recommendation if not even less. The only way that an interview could negatively affect your chances of getting in is if you absolutely bomb your interview and are 100% clueless by failing to demonstrate your academic passion and interest in the school, or by showing up very late, or by not showing up to the interview at all. In all other cases, you're probably fine.

Be Specific in Your Emails

Be prompt in your communication with the interviewer. They will likely contact you by email, and when they do, respond in a timely fashion and give them several available times and places where you are willing to meet (if they don't suggest a location).

Be Early

Plan to show up about 10 minutes early to your interview, and if you arrive early, just chill in your car. Sometimes interviews in the city can make it difficult to find parking, and interviews in obscure locations may be hard to find. Give yourself a nice buffer of time just in case. You don't want to arrive late! If you end up being early, that's fine. Just sit in your car and listen to your favorite song while you go over what you want to mention in your interview.

Prepare Answers to Basic Questions

As far as the majority of the discussion in your interview goes, the alumnus will likely ask some questions about you and then talk about the college that you are applying to. You need to have answers to some standard questions locked and loaded. Just be honest, be attentive, and be prepared to answer questions on all of the following topics:

Why You Want to Go to _____ College

Expect your interviewer to ask you why you want to attend the college that the interview is for. I did eight interviews, and every interviewer opened by asking me that exact question. "So why do you want to go to _____ university when there are so many other great schools?" Be prepared with at least 3 reasons you want to attend. Feel free to make one of the reasons lighthearted, but definitely make sure you have some legitimate reasons for why you want to go. And don't be generic by saying things like "I like the location". Do some research and figure out what you like most about each school before you show up to the interview.

Research the different departments, classes, and professors that may interest you. You can also mention extracurriculars that the school is known for that interest you, special programs that the school has, and why you like certain aspects of the school better than other schools. Do you like the school because they have a great entrepreneurial culture, and you would one day like to start a tech company to help the environment? Does the school have an exceptional comparative literature program with amazing professors and classes that focus on interesting authors and texts? Make sure you really do your research so that you can answer any question possible about your interest in the school.

Your Extracurriculars and Passions

Be able to explain exactly what your specific role was in your favorite activities, why you participated in these activities, what you got out of these activities, and how these activities have shaped your goals and plans for the future. Highlight any major accomplishments or honors that you have received.

What You Do for Fun and Why

This is more important than you think. Think about what you really love that makes you unique. Show the interviewer that you have a life outside of school and extracurriculars.

Your Favorite Book Outside of School

This question is very common, so be prepared with something that isn't Percy Jackson (quality series, but come on, you're not in the 3th grade grade anymore). If Percy Jackson is your answer, it's pretty clear that it must be the only book you've ever read on your own time, and you read it in the 3th grade. That means you haven't read anything independently since the 3rd grade. Not ideal. Be sure to know the basic plot lines and character names from a few of your favorite adult-level books. Also, think about why your favorite book is your favorite.

More Possible Questions

There are a lot more questions your interviewer might ask, but I don't necessarily have any advice on how to answer them other than "be honest". They might ask you about your favorite academic interests, your least favorite classes in high school and why you didn't like them, what you look forward to in college, and what you would change about your high school. As long as you sound reasonably intelligent and tell the truth, you will be fine!

Prepare Your Own Questions

Most interviewers will end the interview by asking if you have any questions. You should have at least three questions prepared or else you will look uninterested in the school. If possible, ask about aspects of the college that you are genuinely interested in, but if you can't think of anything that really interests you, feel free to ask questions like "how hard is it to double major?" or "what was your favorite thing about your college experience?" or "what advice do you have for me going into my freshman year of college?". I can't stress enough that you must have prepared questions. If the interviewer asks if you have any questions, and you say, "ummmmmm…. nope", then it's going to be really awkward, and that's a bad way to end an interview.

Send a Thank You Email

After the interview, send a thank you email (with a proper greeting and closing, of course) to your interviewer later that night. Showing your appreciation for the time that your interviewer spent is a great way to get on his or her good side before he or she submits the interview letter to the college that you are applying to. You don't have to say much, just something along the lines of:

Dear Dr. Smith,

Thank you for taking the time to tell me all about your experience at University of _____ . It was great meeting you today, and through our conversation I learned a lot about why I want to attend University of _____."

Sincerely,

Nathan Halberstadt

Easy enough, right? Just make sure that you have the email locked and loaded so that you can send it the same night as your interview. You don't want your interviewer to write and submit your letter before they see your thank you email.

Section IV: Enjoying Your High School Years

Chapter 13

Cashing in on Summer

Many Summer Programs Are Overrated

Fact: Many summer programs are a waste of your time and money if you are doing them solely to get into college. Of course, there are exceptions, but don't expect that going to Harvard Summer School will help you get into Harvard University. And the same goes for pretty much any other university summer school. That's not to say that these programs don't have value, but the value of the programs is not in their ability to get you into a college. Rather, the value is in the education you get, and perhaps the enjoyment you get from learning.

I never did any summer school or summer programs, and I wouldn't necessarily recommend that you do them either. Many friends of mine who got into top universities never did a summer program, and many friends who did summer programs even at Harvard did not get into any top universities. And yes, if there is a program you really want to do for the sake of doing the program, then go for it! Just don't expect it to necessarily help you get into college.

Start Your Own Business

If you are itching to do something productive with your summer to help you get into a great college, consider this: start a business. You might think that's too hard or not worth it, but it really isn't. Starting a business is probably the single most unique thing you could do to show a college that you are smart, driven, and likely to succeed outside the classroom. And that's what colleges want in a student—driven, smart, and likely to succeed. How many 17-year-olds have done anything major outside the classroom? Most students are too busy watching Netflix, playing Fortnite, and texting friends to ever realize that there are amazing opportunities to innovate at a young age.

I can't stress enough that what you have done outside of the classroom businesswise could be incredibly important to your application. Remember, if you are a high schooler who has started a successful business, it shows colleges that you are industrious. Colleges want people who will go into the real world and run businesses more than they want students who will only get A grades and not do much else.

Work

Let's get real practical here. Whether you are running your own business or employed by somebody else, figure out what you are good at, and start making money doing it. Below are some ideas, but the possibilities are literally endless. You know what you are best at.

- Sell a product. It could be an iphone app, a book, or a gadget of some sort

- Run a repair service. If you know how to repair phone screens, computers, cars, or anything else, you could be in high demand and charge a premium price.

- Create a YouTube channel or podcast with content that will attract viewers, and eventually advertisers, in whatever you know well. Mountain biking? Buy a GoPro and start vlogging. Paintball? Buy a GoPro and start vlogging. Crocheting? Tutorial videos. Fashion? Review products. Legos? Review products or do unboxings. Sports? Start your own sports opinion/commentary channel/podcast. Music? Teach yourself to produce music and record yourself. Art? Drawing tutorials.

- Lawn mowing is much more lucrative than you would think. I ran my own lawn mowing business, and you can make about $30 an hour if you know what you're doing.

- If you are an A+ student, start a tutoring business. Parents are willing to spend a lot of money to help their children succeed, so they will be willing to pay you to tutor their children if you can prove you are capable.

- If you are a musician, start getting paid to be a musician (in pit orchestras or in restaurants or online or by teaching lessons).

- If you are an athlete, start a sports summer camp, or coach a sports team of younger kids, or become a referee.

- Run a STEM or Math camp for students.

- Work at a local store or restaurant. This might not be the most appealing job, but you get real-world experience and get to interact with customers on a daily basis, which will strengthen your interpersonal skills.

- Intern with a company or startup. Getting an internship really varies on what industry you are looking at. Start by contacting your school's career office/guidance department to see if they have any opportunities. However, the best way to get an internship is through connections with the people who you know. See if your parents, family members, teachers, and friends know people at companies that you are interested in and try to get introductions. You can also try cold emailing people. Just make sure that your subject line shows genuine interest and that your email shows exactly why you want to join the company and what skills you would bring to them. You can even do this for professors at local universities if you want to look for a research opportunity over the summer. Tell them why their research interests you and what skills you have. This is where having a résumé and possibly some side projects in your area of interest comes in handy. Also, reach out to startups as they are more likely to take a chance on a younger person. In all communication with companies, indicate your eagerness to learn and grow. If you can land an internship in your area of interest, you will not only get invaluable experience but also a great addition to your college applications.

- Writing. You could work to publish a novel or a book of any kind and even try to sell it on the Amazon KDP store. Just make sure you actually finish the book so that you have an outcome that you can show. "I started writing a book" is not something you want to showcase on your college applications.

- Journalism. You can start your own blog about basically anything—sports, fashion, pop culture, art, literature—just be dedicated. You can even send this work to professional websites through emails or applications to try to get a writing position. Sports journalism, something my editor did, is not too difficult to land a position in, and websites are willing to take chances on young, passionate writers.

- Tech projects. Teach yourself new programming languages and frameworks, and make a project with them. Have you ever wanted to learn Swift to make iPhone apps? How about programming an Amazon Alexa? This is the time to teach yourself new skills! Learn on your own using YouTube, edX, Udemy, W3Schools, or whatever, and use your knowledge to make a project that could turn into a business.

Legit Summer Programs

There are of course some selective summer programs that can be incredible experiences. Below are a few examples but certainly not an exhaustive list.

- RSI (Research Science Institute) accepts only a few students per state, so its very selective, but most of the kids in this program end up going to amazing schools. If you are passionate about science, apply and see how it goes. Getting in will give you a world-class research experience and will allow you to meet some other amazing students. Plus, it will be a huge résumé booster.

- Harvard Summer Business Academy (not to be confused with Harvard Summer School) is an awesome one-week introduction to entrepreneurship. You get to learn the process of starting a company with materials inspired by Harvard Business School, and you get to hear from and meet with many entrepreneurs as well as an HBS professor. You even get to compete in a business pitch competition, after which you can develop your idea into a real business.

- PROMYS at BU is a quality math camp for very talented math students.

- You can look for more in your area. Try to find ones that are actually selective and not just ones where you can pay and get in with no real application process. If they are selective, then they are concerned about getting a talented group of passionate students. This indicates that they want to engage and challenge their students, not just get money from parents. Also, look for programs where you will not only learn and gain experience but also connect with high-performing, like-minded students.

Keep in mind that as great as making money is, the learning experience is what's most important for you in the long run. A great summer job can be the perfect opportunity to show a college that you can work hard, and an academic summer program could also give you the connections that launch you into the business world. So get off Netflix and get busy this summer!

Chapter 14

Sleep in High School

Sleep Makes You Better

I'm no expert on sleep, but I know that in order to be both happy and successful in high school, you need to sleep. Sleep allows your brain to store memories from the day in your long-term memory. Similarly, sleep allows for your body to recover from damage that it sustained during the day through sports, walking, standing, sitting, and the occasional running into things. Sleep has so many health benefits, and it's certainly one of the most underrated academic and athletic "performance enhancing drugs".

If you don't sleep for long enough, you will prevent your brain and body from building back after a tough day. Lack of sleep leads to cognitive and motor impairment in the future, which grows increasingly severe as lack of sleep piles up. This impedes the formation of long-term memory from recent short-term memories. If you don't sleep enough, your brain function becomes similar to that of a drunk person according to a New York Times article (Jones, Maggie. "How Little Sleep Can You Get Away With?" *The New York Times*, 15 Apr. 2011, www.nytimes.com). You would never take an academic test drunk! Yet students take exams on four hours of sleep and then wonder why they fail. They are basically mentally hammered from a lack of sleep.

Unfortunately, high schools tend to start their school days at asininely early times. Many of you may have to wake up around or before 6:00 AM every weekday, which is very tough to sustain, especially if you are juggling many extracurriculars and staying up late doing homework. However, there are several strategies that you can use in order to maximize the amount of rest that you are giving to your body during your hectic high school life.

Get at least 7 hours of sleep. I usually aimed for 8+ hours of sleep in high school, and if I got any less than that it would be a rough day. Everyone's response to sleep is different—some people may feel fine on five hours a day, but remember that in the end it will hurt you. So try to get at least 7 hours of sleep whenever you can even though it may not be possible on some days. You'll definitely be more energized and focused on a daily basis.

Of course, there will be some nights where you will just have to power through on 5 hours of sleep. Sometimes you just can't avoid a late night when you have a tennis match, a few papers to work on, and three tests in the next two days. But most nights are not that busy, and students often go to bed at 1:00 AM on nights when they realistically could have gone to bed at 11:00 PM because they simply aren't as efficient as they should be. Let's face it, we could all do a better job of managing our time, and we are all guilty of procrastinating. Below are some strategies that could help you to increase the amount of time that you sleep.

Don't Save Studying for Later

Start studying for every significant test two nights before the test rather than just doing an all-nighter the night before. Two days before I have a major test, I generally stay up somewhat late and really make sure that I know everything. This way, during the night before the test, I can review some topics quickly then go to bed at a reasonable hour and feel great for the exam. Also, if you do this, you can ask your teachers final questions the day before test.

Let's say you have a test on a Wednesday. This means that most of your studying should be done on Monday afternoon/night. Then on Tuesday, you should talk to your teacher in class and after school to hash out any details you are struggling with. Tuesday night you should go to bed before 11:00 PM because you have already learned what you can. The next morning, you will go into school and do well on the test without because you aren't sleep deprived. It's a win-win. You get a good grade, and you don't get stressed from a lack of sleep.

Nap Time

If you really have a tough time getting to sleep early enough, naps can be a powerful tool. Short naps around 15 minutes in length can help to rejuvenate your brain and allow you to focus better especially while studying. Obviously, naps won't work for everyone (especially if you have trouble falling asleep quickly), but I found them to be an effective way to combine studying and getting rest.

Make Checklists For Yourself

Writing things down is honestly the best way to get things done. Write all of your daily priorities down on a sheet of paper, google document, agenda book, phone, or wherever. When you need something done, put it on the list so that it's not just lingering in your brain and waiting to be forgotten. When you complete a task, cross it off your list. You can choose to organize this checklist however you want; it just needs to make sense to you. This eliminates the time that you waste figuring out what to do and trying to remember all of your priorities. Plus, if you have your list of priorities accessible and easily viewable, you will realize that you need to get going, so you will be less likely to procrastinate.

Use a Schedule

Plan out long-term assignments using a schedule. Again, don't just do this in your head; literally make a schedule. If you have a paper or project due at the end of the week, think about how much you can realistically get done each day given the specific commitments that you have. For example, decide to write a rough draft on Tuesday, to peer edit with a friend on Wednesday, and to finish the final draft on Thursday. Do your best to stick to this schedule. You can always modify it slightly as you go along in order to adapt to unexpected commitments, but as long as you generally stick to it, you will be perfecting your essay when all your friends are nervously starting their opening paragraph.

Discipline Yourself

This is honestly the hardest thing to do. At 10:52 PM on a school night, would you rather get an extra 2 hours of sleep so that you can actually think during tomorrow's physics test, or would you rather binge Netflix and read sports articles and listen to that new album while you text your friends? Instant gratification usually wins in the moment, so you will probably end up texting friends while you jam out. But that's where discipline has to come in. Delayed gratification is the key to success in life. Give up momentary pleasure for your long term good. And yeah, I do sound like your Dad. But trust me, in the long run, sleep and your grades are more important than sports articles and texting your friends.

Power through each task on your to-do list. Then, in between each task, take a break to do something fun. Watch a little TV, get a snack, and maybe even talk to people in your house (I know. Scary.). You need breaks, but make sure this 15-30 min break doesn't turn into a 2 hour break. If you get started with your to-do list right when you get home and don't get carried away with distractions, you should be able to get to bed a reasonable hour. This will take mental discipline and conditioning that only time can develop, but it will make you a much less tired and more satisfied person in the end. Plus, there is always time to have fun on Friday night and over the weekend if you stay focused during the week.

Eliminate Electronic Distractions

Let's be honest. You're a busy person. In fact, you're probably pretty popular. So you spend hours every day after school asserting your dominance in the social hierarchy by scrolling, liking, posting, sending, and receiving electronic content. It's a nice distraction from reality... and that's the problem. It's a distraction. It's impossible to focus while your phone is lighting up with notifications every 17 seconds (oh you social butterfly). Don't use your phone or any social media while you are studying. Turn off your phone or put it in a different room if you have to. Messages that don't relate to school can wait. You'll be fine. And you will be able to go to bed much sooner because you will be more focused.

Falling Asleep

Find something that helps you sleep: some people can fall asleep like a rock the second they put their head on a pillow. For others, sleeping is much harder. To combat this problem, find something that helps you sleep. Feel free to try some of the following suggestions, but everyone is different, so you might have to find something else completely novel that helps you:

- Read something interesting (not school related)
- Read something really boring (probably school related)
- Listen to classical music - there are some great sleep playlists on YouTube
- Listen to a podcast until you get drowsy
- Exercise during the day so that you will be physically tired when you sleep
- Stare at the wall or ceiling (a clear sign of desperation)

Stay Consistent

Don't stay up until 4 AM on Saturday night and then wake up at 12:00 PM on Sunday. This throws off your whole sleep schedule and will mess you up during the school week. Be reasonable about sleep on the weekends (i.e. try not to stay up past 1 AM or sleep in past 10 AM).

Do What Makes You Healthy

Remember that these are only suggestions. I don't know you. Every person is different; we all have different sleep and stress tolerances, and we all react to actions and habits differently. Find what works for you, and don't bother with what others think of your work, sleep, and life habits. As long as they work for you and allow you to be productive, energized, and committed, then you're probably all good.

And while we're in this chapter, I figure I'll throw in a word or two about general health. You should be exercising at least three times a week and eating at least somewhat healthily. Obviously, junk food is amazing, but you have to strike a balance between health food and junk food. You will perform better mentally and physically if you eat better. But in general, sleeping more is an easy change that requires little effort. So if you change just one thing about your lifestyle, SLEEP MORE!

Chapter 15

Having a Life

Focus on What Matters

Don't participate in too many things (i.e. don't try to be in 10 clubs at your school). Instead, give yourself some time to just hang out with friends and do things you love. And you have to have good times. Spend that Friday night watching Netflix with friends. Go out and play some pickup basketball on Sunday afternoon. Spend some quality time at a family dinner. Make sure that you realize that there is more to life than crafting your college applications. Have fun and value the people that give you the most joy in life. If you are grinding away ceaselessly, you will burn out. And even if you are succeeding in your academics, it's not worth the cost to your quality of life.

Get Involved

However, in order to have a life, you need to be involved in things. So when I say "don't participate in too many things", the emphasis is on the "too many" things. If you are doing 15 activities after school, that's too much. But if you are only doing one activity or doing nothing, you need to step up your game. Staying after school to get help from a teacher or talk with friends doesn't count as an activity. I'm talking about getting a job or doing legitimate extracurriculars such as sports, arts, and clubs. Participating in after-school activities will actually help you have a life because you will be practicing and working hard after school with friends. Rather than going home after school and watching YouTube videos all afternoon, you will hopefully be building your skills in a variety of areas. You should pretty easily be able to juggle 2-5 decent after school commitments with a decent amount of success in all of the activities.

Try New Things

Don't be afraid to take risks in high school. Now is the time to try out new and exciting things! After high school, it will start to become too late to learn new activities from scratch. If you have never played golf or volleyball or football but have always wanted to, then go for it in high school. Take advantage of the programs and teams. There are skilled coaches who will teach you what you need to know. The same goes for clubs—you can learn new skills from advisers and older students. Later on in life, that same sort of instruction may not be as easily available. So follow your passions outside of school. Don't let your schoolwork be all you care about. Pursue new and fun activities!

Relax About Your GPA and Test Scores

Don't obsess over your academics and the college process. Nobody wants to be friends with that kid who asks you what grade you got on every test or what your GPA is or what your standardized test scores are or where you are applying to college day in and day out. Don't be that kid. Really. Don't. You will have no friends. There are so many great things to experience in high school. You shouldn't waste all of your time stressing and worrying about the college process. And if you are talking about it all the time, that's a clear indication that you are stressing and worrying about it all the time.

Don't get hung up on websites like College Confidential. The people who post often talk like they are high-achieving, perfect students, but they are probably stretching the truth. Don't trick yourself into thinking that you need to outperform them to get in, or that everyone on the website is as qualified as they talk themselves up to be. It's mostly a waste of time, so stay off the site unless you are looking for the answer to a specific college-related question.

If you get a bad grade, a poor standardized test score, or fail at anything in high school, don't beat yourself up over it too much. Learn from your mistakes and try to do better.

Make the most of the time that you have left right now in high school, and don't worry about mistakes that are in the past. Perhaps those mistakes might affect your admissions decisions, but don't let them affect who you are as a person. Remember, you can be incredibly successful at just about any college, so don't let this process control your happiness.

Chapter 15

Final Timeline

On the pages that follow, I'm going to lay out a rough sketch of what you should be doing in high school at each different stage. Obviously, not every student will be able to follow this schedule exactly, but hopefully you find it helpful for staying on the right track.

Freshman Year

Fall	Winter	Spring	Summer (Different Options)
Play a sport	Narrow down your extracurriculars to 2-5 major ones	Continue the extracurriculars that you are enjoying	Work/Intern
Try something in the arts	Get good grades	Take SAT Subject Test (if possible)	Teach yourself something new
Try a bunch of clubs		Get good grades	Travel
Explore any and all activities that you think you may be interested in			Attend a valuable and interesting summer program
Get good grades			Start a Business

Sophomore Year

Fall	Winter	Spring	Summer (Different Options)
Continue extracurriculars and explore new ones if they interest you	Start asserting your dominance in your chosen extracurriculars	Run for leadership positions in your extracurriculars	Work/Intern
Take PSAT/NMSQT	Get good grades	Take SAT Subject Test (if possibly)	Start a business
Get good grades		Get good grades	Attend a valuable and interesting summer program
		Make résumé	Teach yourself something new
			Travel

Junior Year ("Get Good Grades" is implied)

August	Prepare for PSAT/NMSQT	Start looking at colleges
September	Prepare for PSAT/NMSQT	Apply to National Honor Society
October	Take PSAT/NMSQT	Prepare for/take SAT/ACT
November	Prepare for/take SAT/ACT	Figure out which colleges you may be interested in visiting
December	Prepare for/take SAT/ACT	Visit colleges
January	Prepare for/take SAT/ACT	Visit colleges
February	Prepare for/take SAT/ACT	Visit colleges
March	Prepare for/take SAT/ACT	Survive
April	Prepare for/take SAT/ACT	Prepare for AP exams and subject tests
May	Prepare for/take SAT/ACT	Take AP exams and SAT Subject Tests
June	Take SAT/ACT	Ask teachers for letters of recommendation
July	Start brainstorming Common App Essay	Visit colleges and decide which colleges to apply to

Senior Year ("Get Good Grades" is implied)

Note: Apply for any and all scholarships throughout the year

| August | Finalize list of colleges you will apply to | Fill out the general information on Common App

Continue Working on Common App Essay |
| --- | --- | --- |
| September | Complete all early action/decision supplements

Request Transcripts to be sent to Colleges | Make sure letters of recommendation are submitted

Continue Working on Common App Essay/Information |
| October | Submit Early Action/Decision Applications by November 1 (or the applicable deadline) | Complete and submit FAFSA and CSS profile (and look for additional financial aid deadlines)

Finalize Common App Essay/Information |
November	Work on all regular decision supplements	Early Action/Decision Interviews
December	Submit Regular Decision Applications by early January (or the applicable deadline)	Hear Back from Early Applications
January	Interviews	Maintain your grades
February	Interviews	Maintain your grades
March	Notification of admissions decision	Maintain your grades
April	Decide on college and put deposit down (by May 1)	Maintain your grades
May	Submit college forms	Maintain your grades
June	Submit college forms	Get ready for college!
July	Submit college forms	Get ready for college!

The Long Term Plan

If you generally follow these schedules, you will run into minimal trouble along the way. Just make sure you are getting things done early rather than at the last minute. You don't want to be submitting your college applications at 11:54 PM on January 1st 6 minutes before they are due. If you start early enough, turning them in a week or two early would be a great idea. New Year's Day isn't the time to be frantickly slapping together your college applications.

If you put the work in, you will do well in high school, in college, and in all of your future pursuits. Don't let anybody or anything hold you back. Reach for your dreams! Be bold and don't settle for mediocrity.

I hope that you found this book helpful. If you did, could you do me a big favor and write an honest review on Amazon so that others can discover this book? I'd really appreciate the feedback! And definitely check out my other book, *New SAT Strategies for a 1600,* if you are looking to improve your SAT score. It's the most helpful, concise, and straight-to-the-point SAT prep book out there. I've received lots of positive feedback from it, and I guarantee that you will find the book very helpful. Also, feel free to email me with any questions at nathan.halberstadt@gmail.com. I love to hear from my readers! If you want to hear more from me, you can follow me on Instagram at n8halberstadt. Thanks!

Good luck with everything. Onward!